Kerry

Written by Marie Farré
Illustrated by Jean-Pierre Moreau

Specialist adviser: Steve Pollock,
The British Museum
(Natural History)

ISBN 1 85103 001 8
First published 1986 in the United Kingdom by
Moonlight Publishing Ltd.,
131 Kensington Church Street, London W8

POCKET • WORLDS

Bees, Ants and Termites

Why do some insects
live together?

Have you watched a bee flying from flower to flower? Mind it doesn't sting you!

A bee drinking nectar

Have you ever given ants a feast of a teaspoonful of sugar? They love it!

Have you ever seen a termite? Perhaps not – they live in warm countries, hidden in old wood.

Ants

Great big families

All these insects, ants, termites, honey-bees, are called **social insects** because they live in social groups – they can't survive on their own. The groups are like little countries, with a queen, soldiers and workers. How do members of the same group recognise each other? By smell!

A termite and its nest

Thanks to the tiny claws on their feet, bees can walk upside down on the ceiling.

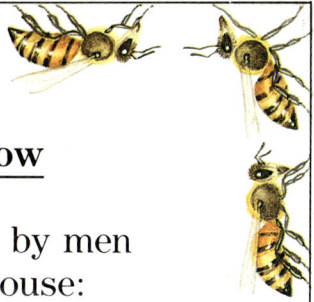

Wild bees live in hollow tree-trunks.

The domestic bees kept by men live in a little wooden house: a **beehive.**

A beehive has 50,000 inhabitants, as many as a small town.
Nearly all the bees are workers. During their lives, they take turns to be nurses, builders, housekeepers, food-carriers, soldiers... Their bodies are well suited to their work. When they are nurses, they produce royal jelly. And when the bees carry food in from the surrounding flowers, they put it in special sacs on their legs and stomachs.

There aren't many males. They don't sting, don't work – and don't even know how to feed themselves!

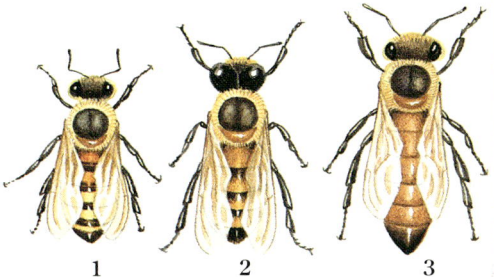

1. Worker
2. Male or drone
3. Queen

1   2   3

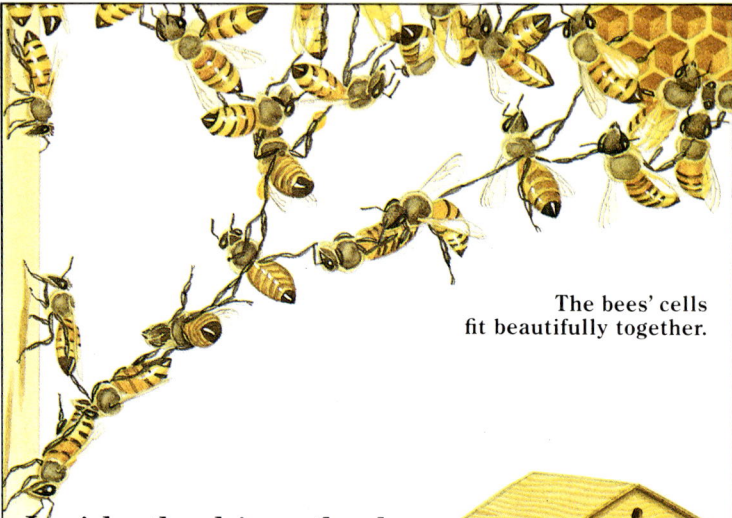

The bees' cells fit beautifully together.

Inside the hive, the bees build cells made of wax. **Where does the wax come from?**

The workers have to eat a lot of honey to make the wax – about 10lbs of honey for 1lb of wax! It is produced in tiny flakes below their stomachs. They soften the wax by chewing it, then shape it into cells. The workers always keep the hive clean. In hot weather they even cool it by beating their wings!

The beekeeper collects the honey from the frame.

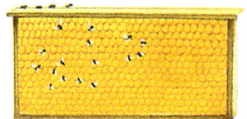

There are lots of different kinds of hives all over the world: wooden hives,

hives made out of tree-trunks, covered with a flat stone,

hives of straw, and even multi-storey hives!

The queen is the mother of all the bees in the hive.

Surrounded by workers, she lays thousands of eggs, day and night. The eggs are placed in the tiny wax cells. After three days, the larvae develop from the eggs. They are fed by the workers on the same food as all the bees eat – a mixture of pollen and honey.

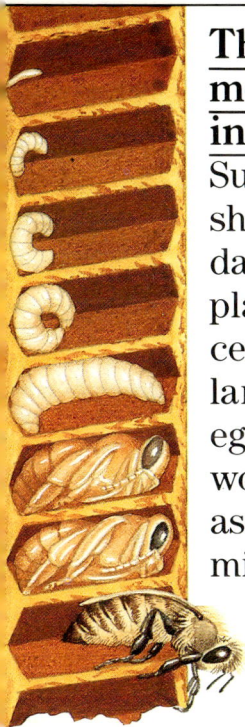

You can see here how the egg develops into the larva, which grows into a bee.

Future queens eat special food.

They are fed on royal jelly, a rich mixture made specially for them. The queens live for five years – a worker bee for about six weeks.

This damp bee has just come out of the cell for the first time!

The buzzing bee flits from flower to flower.

Is it feeding itself? No, it is collecting pollen, the fine yellow powder, and nectar, the sweet liquid, from flowers.

They put the nectar and pollen in special sacs to carry them back to the hive – the nectar by their stomach, the pollen on their legs. The nectar is used to make honey.

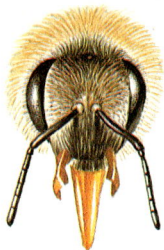

The bee sucks up the nectar with its long probing tongue.

It fixes the pollen to sacs on its back legs.

Bees' eyes are different from ours, and they see colours differently. This is probably what the colours of the flowers on the opposite page look like to a bee.

Heather   Clover   Mint   Rosemary   Lavender

Bees make dozens of journeys backwards and forwards to the hive every day!

They find their direction from the way the light falls in the sky. When they get back to the hive, they tell the other bees where they have found their nectar, by dancing! If they dance round in a circle, it means the flowers are less than 100 metres away. If they dance in a figure eight, the flowers are further off...
Dancing is the bees' way of talking. When the bee has handed over its load of nectar and pollen to the workers at the hive, it sets off to fetch more.

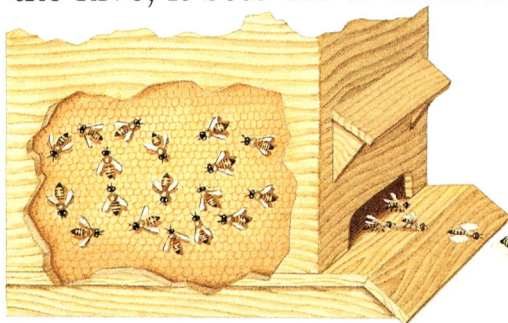

| Lime | Acacia | Chestnut | Pine | Thyme |

How do bees make honey?

They have to get rid of the water in the nectar, so they beat their wings over it to make the water evaporate. The nectar gets stickier and stickier. When it is a thick paste, the bee chews it up, and puts it away in a cell. There it soon turns into honey.

The taste of the honey depends on the flowers the nectar came from. There are all sorts of different flavours of honey.

The worker stores the pollen by ramming it down into the cell with its head.

How do beekeepers collect the honey?

Before collecting the honey, the beekeepers make the bees sleepy by puffing smoke into the hive. Then they lift the roof off the hive and collect the frames of honey. During one season, they may collect 35 big jars full. But they are always careful to leave enough for the bees to live on through the winter.

What do bees do when the cold weather comes?

They huddle together inside the hive and spend a slow, sleepy time, feeding off their summer supplies. No more work is done by the workers, the queen lays no more eggs. If they haven't got enough honey, the beekeeper feeds them sugar to keep them going.

The beekeeper scrapes the frame to take off the top covering of wax.

This beekeeper has placed the queen bee on his chin – all the other bees have gathered round her, and hang there, like a buzzing beard!

What happens when there are too many bees in the hive?

A wild swarm

As the queen lays more and more eggs, more and more bees develop. When the hive is too crowded, the bees swarm. The old queen flies off, and half the bees from the hive follow her. If a beekeeper finds them, he pops them in a new hive.

In the old hive, a new queen wakes up. She kills the other females and flies out of the hive to mate with the drones. Then she returns to lay eggs...

The beekeeper encourages the bees into the hive.

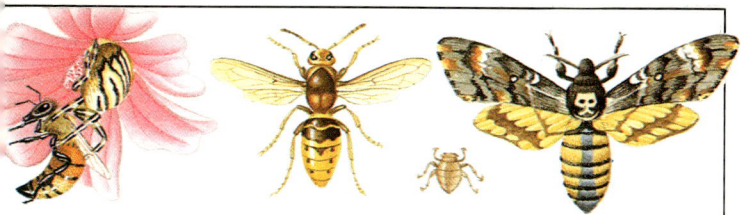

A bee has enemies:

spiders   hornets   fleas   death's head
                                                   moth

Not only bees — and people — like honey.

But the bees are there, on guard, with their weapons at the ready! They are prepared to sting anybody who disturbs the hive: wasps, hornets, bees from other hives, even bears and badgers...

And what if a mouse slips into the hive?

The angry bees quickly sting it to death. But its body is too heavy for the bees to push it out. If it stays there, though, it will soon rot and smell horrible. So the bees cover it with a special paste, propolis, which dries the mouse-body out without letting it rot!

The workers also use propolis to waterproof things. They make it from the sticky resin on the surface of flower-buds.

The young queen ants fly off.

Scurry, scurry, scurry go the ants...

Like bees, they have a queen, workers and soldiers. But they live longer than bees: the workers live two years, while the queen can live up to twenty years. In midsummer, the young queens fly away. They each find their own hole, shed their wings, and crawl inside to lay their eggs. In a few weeks, the larvae hatch out, become ants and begin making the nest bigger, building tunnels and rooms using twigs, saliva and moss. They dig special rooms for their larders and nurseries. The eggs, larvae and cocoons each have their special places. They even make doors which they shut at night!

1   2   3

1. Worker
2. Male
3. Queen

If you see a little pile of twigs in the forest, don't tread on it – it might be the roof of an ants' nest!

A grasshopper being eaten by ants.

What do ants eat? Seeds, leaves, fruit – and other insects. They love the sweet liquid given off by greenfly, and will keep them specially so as to 'milk' them! **What does an ant do when it finds a grasshopper too big for it to carry?** It calls its friends. It leaves little drops of scent along its trail, which carry a signal for other ants saying 'come and help!'. Ants have a whole language of smells – some mean 'danger!', some 'feed the queen!'...

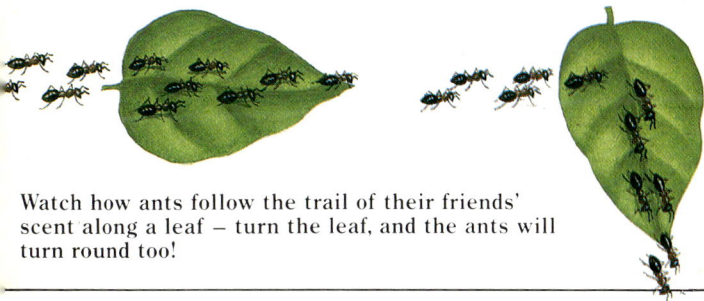

Watch how ants follow the trail of their friends' scent along a leaf – turn the leaf, and the ants will turn round too!

These **Australian ants** have collected honeydew and stored it in their stomachs. They hang upside down, and other ants share their honey when food is scarce.

Did you know there are over 6,000 kinds of ants?

Tailor ants from Asia work as a team to make a nest out of leaves – they sew the leaves together with silky thread produced by their grubs. African army ants are fierce and hungry – they will eat anything that doesn't get out of their way fast enough. You can see them here just starting to eat a snake.

These parasol ants from South America cut down leaves and take them into their nests, where they grow mushrooms on them!

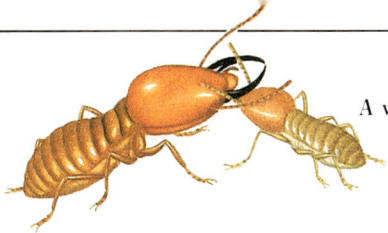
A worker termite feeds a soldier.

What is white and blind and eats wood?

A termite. Termites hardly ever leave their nests. If they do, the air dries their bodies and could kill them. In hot countries, they build huge nests out of mud and saliva that can tower taller than a man. Inside the nests, hundreds of tunnels lead out to the store-rooms. There they keep twigs, leaves, bits of old wood...

Right in the middle of the nest lies the enormous, swollen queen. She can't move, and simply lays egg after egg, waited on by her little king, and the busy band of workers.

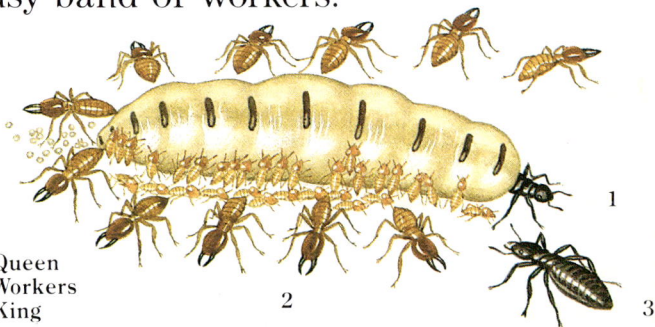

1. Queen
2. Workers
3. King

There are termites in Europe too.

They keep mostly to the south of Europe, and there are none in Britain. They do a lot of damage. Look at what they have done to the house opposite by eating away at the roof-timbers! In Europe, termites live in the wood of dead and dying trees, or in house-timbers. They chew the wood, and dig tunnels to make their nests. Even concrete doesn't stop them – they just go round it!

The powerful jaws of a worker

Termites talk to each other by tapping on wood!

It's a bit like morse code! When there is danger, they tap on the wood, and then everyone knows to rush back to the nest.

Paper is made of wood – and termites love eating paper too! Sometimes they'll leave only the cover on a book!

Wasp

Bee

Bumblebee

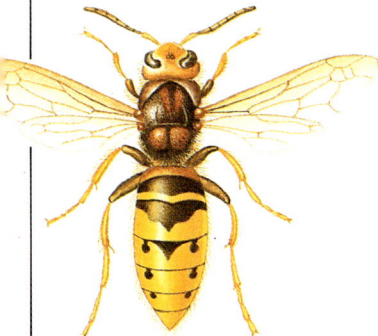

Hornet

True or false?

A wasp is bigger
than a bee.
False.

If you are stung by a
bee, rub the place.
False. You'll rub the
sting in if you do. But
if you get tweezers, and
edge them between the
sting and the poison-sac,
you can pull the
sting out without
spreading the poison.

A bee can fly
at 25km an hour.
True.

Ants are no good.
False. By churning
up the soil, they help
air get to the roots
of plants.

A big ants' nest can eat ten thousand insects in a day. **True.**

Ants sting.
True and **false.** Only some ants sting. The ones that can really hurt you mostly live in hot countries.

Soldier termites spray poison. **True.** They have poison-glands on their foreheads, and some can spray a special rubber, like chewing-gum, which clogs up their enemies.

Index

ants, 7, 24-29, 34-35
army ants, 29
beekeepers, 18-21
bees, 7, 9-23, 34
beeswax, 10
dancing, 16
drones, 9
greenfly, 27
hives, 9-11
honey, 17-18, 29
honeydew ants, 29

hornets, 23
language, 16, 27, 33
nectar, 13, 15
nests, 24, 30, 35
nurseries, 9, 13, 24, 30
parasol ants, 29
pollen, 13, 15
propolis, 23
queen ants, 24
queen bee, 9, 13, 21
queen termite, 30

royal jelly, 13
stings, 7, 27, 34-35
swarms, 21
tailor ants, 29
termites, 7, 30-33
wasps, 23, 34
worker ants, 24
worker bees, 9